PBR

A Pillar Box Red Publication

in association with

MATCH!
THE BEST FOOTBALL MAGAZINE!

ISBN: 978-1-907823-54-1

Photographs: © Getty Images.

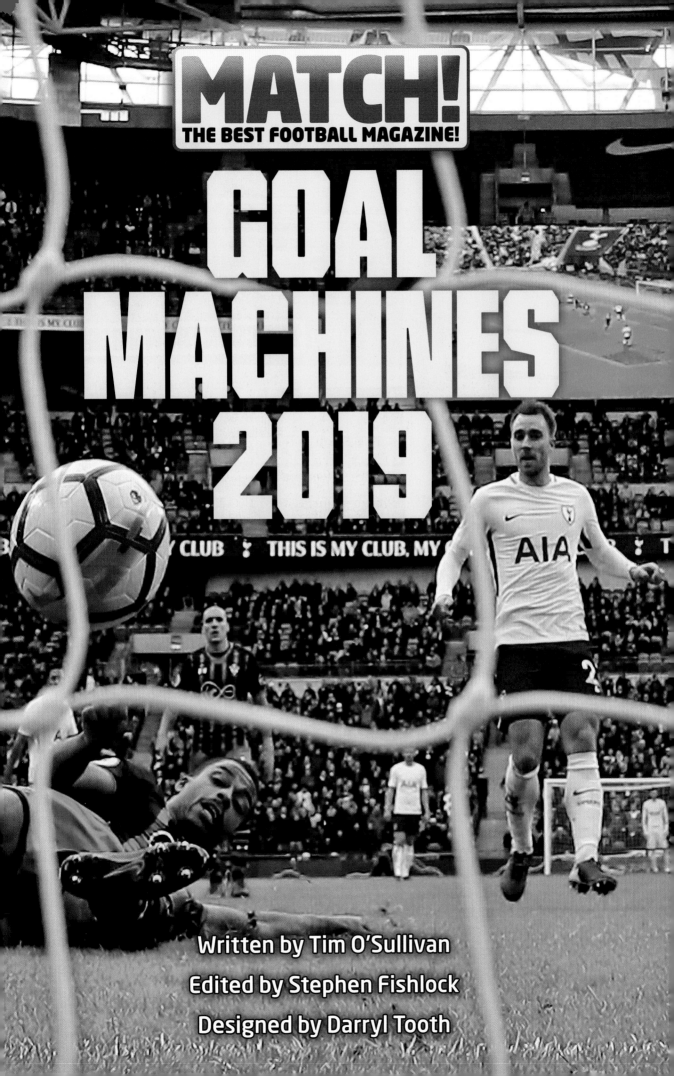

MATCH!
THE BEST FOOTBALL MAGAZINE!

GOAL MACHINES 2019

Written by Tim O'Sullivan

Edited by Stephen Fishlock

Designed by Darryl Tooth

THE COUNTDOWN BEGINS 8

Moussa Dembele — 100 — Club: Lyon DOB: 12/7/96 Country: France
Arjen Robben — 99 — Club: B. Munich DOB: 23/1/84 Country: Holland
Karl Toko Ekambi — 96 — Club: Villarreal DOB: 14/9/92 Country: Cameroon
Talisca — 95 — Club: Guangzhou Evergrande Country: Brazil DOB: 1/2/94
Emmanuel Adebayor — 98 — Club: Istanbul Basaksehir Country: Togo
Wayne Rooney — 97 — Club: DC United DOB: 24/10/85 Country: England
Alassane Plea — 94 — Club: B. Monchengladbach Country: France DOB: 10/3/93

STAT ATTACK!
PREMIER LEAGUE

PREM STAT ATTACK 14

31 — 3 — 32 — 1 — 10 — 4 — 2 — 141 — 177 — 4

EPIC QUIZZES 28 & 48

QUIZ 2

FOOTY MIS-MATCH
Check out these two pics, then see if you can spot the ten differences between them!

GOAL MACHINES BRAIN-BUSTER
Can you pick up a perfect score in our goal machines quiz?

CL STAT ATTACK 20

WIN EPIC FOOTY BOOTS 58

WORLD CUP STAT ATTACK 42

Moussa Dembele

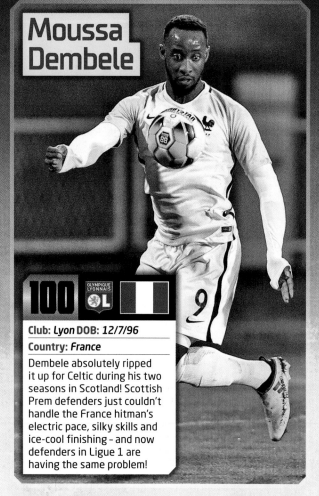

100 | OLYMPIQUE LYONNAIS

Club: *Lyon* **DOB:** *12/7/96*

Country: *France*

Dembele absolutely ripped it up for Celtic during his two seasons in Scotland! Scottish Prem defenders just couldn't handle the France hitman's electric pace, silky skills and ice-cool finishing – and now defenders in Ligue 1 are having the same problem!

Arjen Robben

99 | FC BAYERN MÜNCHEN

Club: *B. Munich* **DOB:** *23/1/84*

Country: *Holland*

We reckon Robben is one of the best wingers in footy history! Experts on TV always think defenders should stop him turning onto his left foot and scoring, but it's easier said than done! His lightning pace, mind-boggling skill and lethal left foot are epic to watch!

Emmanuel Adebayor

98 | B

Club: *Istanbul Basaksehir*

Country: *Togo* **DOB:** *26/2/84*

Adebayor is currently busting nets for Turkish side Istanbul Basaksehir, but he's previously played for Euro giants Real Madrid, Arsenal, Man. City and Monaco. He scored 24 Premier League goals in 2007-08 and is still beating goalkeepers for fun ten years later. Awesome!

Wayne Rooney

97 | D.C. UNITED

Club: *DC United* **DOB:** *24/10/85*

Country: *England*

Wazza is a proper legend of the game! Rooney started his career with Everton, before moving on to Man. United and winning five league titles. He's the Premier League's second all-time top goalscorer in history and is now ripping up the MLS with DC United!

Karl Toko Ekambi

96

Club: Villarreal **DOB:** 14/9/92

Country: Cameroon

The classy Cameroon striker was a breakout star of Ligue 1 in 2017-18. Ekambi smashed in 17 league goals for Angers, including strikes against Lyon, PSG and Nice. The 26-year-old's elite finishing skills helped earn him a big move to La Liga with Spanish side Villarreal!

Talisca

95

Club: Guangzhou Evergrande

Country: Brazil **DOB:** 1/2/94

Talisca has been a promising midfielder for years, but he's added goals to his game the last two seasons. He netted 14 league goals for Besiktas in 2017-18, plus four more in the Champions League, before making a shock loan move to China earlier this summer!

Alassane Plea

94

Club: B. Monchengladbach

Country: France **DOB:** 10/3/93

Plea has been one of the most consistent and lethal forwards in Ligue 1 over the past couple of years. He scored 11 league goals for Nice in 2016-17, then another 16 in 2017-18. His epic pace and finishing earned him a summer move to German team Borussia Monchengladbach!

Hirving Lozano

93 PSV 🇲🇽

Club: *PSV Eindhoven*

Country: *Mexico* **DOB:** *30/7/95*

Lozano was the star of the show as PSV won their 24th Eredivisie title in 2017-18. The Mexico winger stunned every team and fan in Holland with his dynamite dribbling and sensational finishing. He scored 17 league goals, then rocked the World Cup!

Robin van Persie

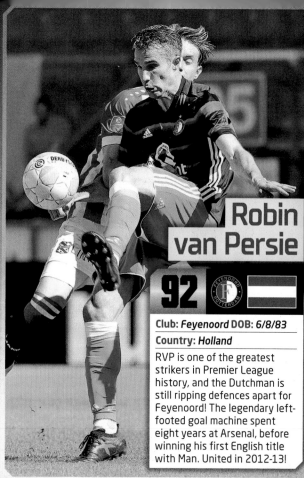

92 F 🇳🇱

Club: *Feyenoord* **DOB:** *6/8/83*

Country: *Holland*

RVP is one of the greatest strikers in Premier League history, and the Dutchman is still ripping defences apart for Feyenoord! The legendary left-footed goal machine spent eight years at Arsenal, before winning his first English title with Man. United in 2012-13!

Anthony Martial

91 🔴 🇫🇷

Club: *Man. United*

Country: *France* **DOB:** *5/12/95*

It feels like Martial has been around forever, but he's still in his early 20s! The speedy France attacker scored vital winning goals against Spurs and Burnley in 2017-18, and has all the ability to become a world-class superstar in 2019!

Aleksandar Mitrovic

90 F 🇷🇸

Club: *Fulham* **DOB:** *16/9/94*

Country: *Serbia*

The Serbia striker's career has been a bit up and down, but he went on an absolute goals explosion during an awesome loan spell at Fulham in 2018! Mitrovic helped them reach the Premier League with 12 goals in 15 starts, and now he's there permanently!

Ashley Barnes

89

Club: *Burnley* **DOB:** *30/10/89*

Country: *Austria*

Unsung hero Barnes had his best ever season in 2017-18. The energetic striker scored in Burnley's 2-2 shock draw with Man. United, the 3-0 win away to West Ham, the winner against Stoke and loads more in a wicked season for The Clarets. His work-rate rules!

Riyad Mahrez

88

Club: *Man. City* **DOB:** *21/2/91*

Country: *Algeria*

Mahrez can be one of the most devastating goalscoring wingers on the planet when he's on top form. The 2015-16 PFA Player Of The Year has a similar playing style to Holland legend Arjen Robben, with tricky dribbling, sick free-kicks and a devastating left foot!

Aaron Ramsey

87

Club: *Arsenal* **DOB:** *26/12/90*

Country: *Wales*

Gunners superstar Ramsey is the new Frank Lampard in the Prem — making late runs into the 18-yard box and punishing defenders with his intelligent movement. Rambo has scored winning goals in two FA Cup finals, including a brilliant header against Chelsea!

Quincy Promes

86

Club: *Sevilla* **DOB:** *4/1/92*

Country: *Holland*

Speedster Promes really burst onto the European football scene in 2017-18 with a series of eye-popping performances for Spartak Moscow. The Dutch wing wizard won the Russian Premier League top goalscorer prize, before sealing a dream £18 million move to Sevilla!

Munas Dabbur

85

Club: *Red Bull Salzburg*

Country: *Israel* **DOB:** *14/5/92*

Dabbur was the top scorer in the Austrian Bundesliga last season with a mega 22 goals! The deadly Israel striker also found the net five times as Red Bull Salzburg reached the semi-finals of the Europa League. His electric pace and lethal finishing are awesome!

Glenn Murray

84

Club: *Brighton* **DOB:** *25/9/83*

Country: *England*

Murray is a proper golden oldie compared to most players in this Top 100 list, but he proves that age is nowhere near as important as football ability. The class Seagulls striker loves to boss Prem defenders with his aerial strength, awesome power and clever movement!

Fabio Quagliarella

83

Club: *Sampdoria*

Country: *Italy* **DOB:** *31/1/83*

Quagliarella rolled back the years in 2017-18 with 19 league goals for Sampdoria! The 35-year-old hitman has been busting Serie A nets for years and won three titles at Juventus, but now he's using his clever finishing skills to push Sampdoria up the table!

Raphinha

82

Club: *Sporting* **DOB:** *14/12/96*

Country: *Brazil*

Raphinha is defo one to watch in 2019! The Brazil wonderkid became a big name in Portugal in 2017-18 after bossing it for Vitoria Guimaraes. He totally stunned the Primeira Liga with 15 league goals, then got a huge move to Lisbon giants Sporting in the summer!

Alireza Jahanbakhsh

81

Club: *Brighton* **DOB:** *11/8/93*

Country: *Iran*

Jahanbakhsh joined an elite list of stars to win the Eredivisie top scorer prize after bagging 21 goals for AZ Alkmaar in 2017-18! The Iran winger has dynamite dribbling skills, but improved his finishing in 2018 to become the total package – and Brighton's record signing!

STAT ATTACK!

31

Before he became a global superstar at Real Madrid and Juventus, Cristiano Ronaldo won a Premier League Golden Boot with Man. United. The Portugal legend netted 31 goals in 2007-08!

3

Man. City goal king Sergio Aguero was the only star to bag three Premier League hat-tricks in 2017-18. What a total legend!

4

Mohamed Salah and Sergio Aguero both scored four goals in a single Prem game in 2017-18. Salah's four were against Watford, while Aguero smashed four past Leicester!

10

There were ten Prem hat-tricks in 2017-18, but Bournemouth ace Callum Wilson was the only player to score one with a team who finished in the bottom half of the table!

141

Harry Kane became the second fastest player to score 100 Prem goals recently. The Tottenham ace hit 100 in 141 games, but Alan Shearer still holds the record after doing it in 124 games!

4

Four net-busters scored 20 or more Prem goals in 2017-18 – Mohamed Salah, Harry Kane, Sergio Aguero and Jamie Vardy. Heroes!

2

Only two of the ten highest Prem scorers of all-time were still playing in 2017-18. Second-placed Wayne Rooney and seventh-placed Jermain Defoe!

32

Mohamed Salah broke the all-time record for most goals in a 38-game Prem season, with 32 strikes for Liverpool in 2017-18!

1

Aaron Ramsey was the only midfielder to score a Prem hat-trick in 2017-18. The Arsenal hero netted an epic treble against Everton!

4

Between the 2000-01 and 2005-06 seasons, Arsenal legend Thierry Henry won the Prem Golden Boot four times! He finished second and third in the other two seasons. Sick!

177

Chelsea legend Frank Lampard is the fourth highest Premier League scorer of all time with 177 goals. He's also the only midfielder in the top 15. Crazy!

Odsonne Edouard

80

Club: *Celtic* **DOB:** *16/1/98*

Country: *France*

The France wonderkid joined Celtic on loan from PSG last season and became an instant fans' favourite. Edouard is just 20, but he's already showing signs of becoming a star with epic power and quick feet. His double against Rangers in April showcased his raw talent!

Javier Hernandez

79

Club: *West Ham* **DOB:** *1/6/88*

Country: *Mexico*

Chicharito has enjoyed an epic career and is definitely one of the most natural finishers the game has seen over the past ten years! The Mexico legend busted nets for Man. United, Real Madrid and Leverkusen, before helping The Hammers avoid relegation in 2017-18!

Andrea Belotti

78

Club: *Torino* **DOB:** *20/12/93*

Country: *Italy*

Belotti looks set to become a footy superstar in 2019! The lethal Torino striker scored 36 Serie A goals in 2017-18 and 2016-17 combined, which has got all the biggest clubs in Europe scouting him. His mix of power, agility and red-hot finishing is tough to stop!

Burak Yilmaz

77

Club: *Trabzonspor*

Country: *Turkey* **DOB:** *15/7/85*

Burak Yilmaz has been busting nets for Turkish teams most of his career and now he's doing it for giants Trabzonspor. The 33-year-old goal king doesn't have blistering pace or mega power, but he's awesome at making intelligent runs and finishing like an ice-cool king!

Wilfried Zaha

76

Club: *C. Palace* **DOB:** *10/11/92*

Country: *Ivory Coast*

Zaha had his best ever season in front of goal in 2017-18. The trick-loving wing wizard has always been famous for bamboozling full-backs with his incredible dribbling skills, but Eagles boss Roy Hodgson encouraged him to shoot more and Zaha delivered in style!

Willian Jose

75

Club: *Real Sociedad*

Country: *Brazil* **DOB:** *23/11/91*

Willian Jose hit double figures in La Liga for the second season in a row in 2017-18! Real Sociedad's ace Brazilian scored 15 goals in Spain's top flight, including net-busters against Barcelona and Atletico Madrid. His movement is so clever and his finishing rules!

Leon Bailey

74

Club: *Bayer Leverkusen*
Country: *Jamaica* **DOB:** *9/8/97*

There aren't many footy stars under the age of 21 who are better than Jamaican-born ace Bailey! The rapid winger mixes epic pace with silky dribbling skills to make him a defender's worst nightmare! He added goals to his game in 2017-18, with nine Bundesliga strikes!

Charlie Austin

73

Club: *Southampton*
Country: *England* **DOB:** *5/7/89*

Deadly hitman Austin is one of the most clinical finishers in English footy! Injuries slowed down his season in 2017-18, but he helped The Saints avoid relegation with goals v West Ham, Everton and Arsenal. His movement and ability to sniff out chances totally rule!

Maxi Gomez

72

Club: *Celta Vigo* **DOB:** *14/8/96*
Country: *Uruguay*

Spanish giants Celta Vigo snapped up Maxi Gomez from Defensor Sporting in 2017 and the young striker made an instant impact in European football. Gomez netted 17 La Liga goals in his debut season, including a strike at the Nou Camp against Barcelona!

Leroy Sane

71

Club: *Man. City DOB: 11/1/96*

Country: *Germany*

Sane arrived at Man. City as a speedy winger with bags of tricks, but boss Pep Guardiola helped him find his shooting boots and now the Germany international is becoming the total package! Sane scored ten Prem goals in 2017-18, including two past Liverpool!

Christian Eriksen

70

Club: *Tottenham DOB: 14/2/92*

Country: *Denmark*

Eriksen started his career as a crafty playmaker with bags of assists in his locker, but his all-round game has improved and now he knows where the net is too! He helped Denmark reach the 2018 World Cup with a hat-trick against Republic of Ireland in the play-offs!

Kevin Volland

68

Club: *Bayer Leverkusen*

Country: *Germany DOB: 30/7/92*

The 26-year-old goal machine has improved every year since bursting onto the scene back in 2010-11. Volland netted 14 Bundesliga goals last season, including a hat-trick against Eintracht Frankfurt and top strikes against Bayern Munich, Dortmund and RB Leipzig!

Memphis Depay

69

Club: *Lyon DOB: 13/2/94*

Country: *Holland*

Memphis was the next big thing when he was a teenager and is now starting to prove the hype was real after a poor spell with Man. United. The Holland speedster was the third top scorer in Ligue 1 last season, with 19 goals for French giants Lyon!

STAT ATTACK!

4

Robert Lewandowski is the only player in history to score four goals in a Champions League semi-final! He did it for former club Borussia Dortmund against Real Madrid back in 2012-13!

10

Liverpool superstars Sadio Mane, Roberto Firmino and Mohamed Salah all scored exactly ten goals each in the 2017-18 CL season!

7

Lionel Messi had scored 100 Champions League goals and bagged seven hat-tricks by the end of 2017-18. What a legend!

6

Cristiano Ronaldo's won the Champions League top scorer award seven times, including the last six seasons in a row! He's a total goal machine!

10.12

Ex-Bayern Munich striker Roy Makaay scored the fastest ever Champions League goal with a strike against Real Madrid after just 10.12 seconds!

17

CR7 holds the record for most CL goals in a single season with 17 in 2013-14. He's also second and third in that list with 16 in 2015-16 and 15 in 2017-18!

3

Wayne Rooney scored an epic hat-trick on his Champions League debut for Man. United against Turkish side Fenerbahce in 2004-05!

100

Back in 2017, Cristiano Ronaldo became the first player to score 100 Champions League goals. The following year he was the first to score 100 in the competition for the same club – Real Madrid. Sick!

5

Only two players have ever scored five goals in a single Champions League game. Luiz Adriano did it for Shakhtar Donetsk against BATE Borisov and the great Lionel Messi hit five past Bayer Leverkusen!

2

Croatia striker Mario Mandzukic has scored in two Champions League finals for two different clubs. He found the net for Bayern Munich in 2013 and Juventus in 2017!

1

Layvin Kurzawa did something his PSG team-mates Cavani, Mbappe and Neymar couldn't do in 2017-18 – that's score a Champo League hat-trick. He's a left-back... wowzers!

Nabil Fekir

67 OLYMPIQUE LYONNAIS L

Club: Lyon **DOB:** 18/7/93

Country: France

Fekir has always been famous for silky dribbling and wicked tricks, but he added goals to his game in 2017-18. The Lyon playmaker netted 18 times in Ligue 1, including a strike in a shock 2-1 win against PSG. His ice-cool playing style could help him become a superstar!

Bas Dost

65 SCP SPORTING

Club: Sporting **DOB:** 31/5/89

Country: Holland

Dost has busted tons of nets in Holland and Germany, and now he's leaving fans speechless in Portugal! The 29-year-old hit a jaw-dropping 27 league goals for Sporting in 2017-18 - that after bagging 34 times the season before! Defenders can't handle his monster strength!

Philippe Coutinho

66 FCB

Club: Barcelona **DOB:** 12/6/92

Country: Brazil

Arguably the best long-range shooter in the world, Coutinho is rapidly turning into a major goal threat! He scored seven goals for Liverpool in 2017-18, before moving to Barcelona in January and netting eight La Liga strikes in just 16 starts!

Gerard Moreno

64 CV

Club: Villarreal **DOB:** 7/4/92

Country: Spain

Moreno scored an awesome 16 La Liga goals for Espanyol in 2017-18! The Villarreal ace rejoined his boyhood club in the summer for £20 million after a successful spell at Espanyol, and is in the best form of his career right now. His movement is awesome!

Wissam Ben Yedder

63

Club: *Sevilla* **DOB:** *12/8/90*

Country: *France*

Ben Yedder hasn't hit fewer than nine league goals in a season since 2011-12! The consistent France ace enjoyed another brilliant season in 2017-18, including a dramatic double against Man. United in the Champions League. His away goals for Sevilla knocked The Red Devils out of Europe!

Mark Uth

62

Club: *Schalke* **DOB:** *24/8/91*

Country: *Germany*

Uth earned a free transfer to Schalke in the summer after a top Bundesliga season with surprise packages Hoffenheim. The 27-year-old netted 14 league goals in 2017-18 to help his side earn a shock top-four finish in Germany!

Vincent Aboubakar

61

Club: *Porto* **DOB:** *22/1/92*
Country: *Cameroon*

Aboubakar used his immense strength and finishing skills to score 15 Primeira Liga goals for Porto in 2017-18! The Cameroon ace mixes monster power with clever movement, so he's an absolute nightmare for defenders! He overpowers centre-backs for fun. Hero!

Marko Arnautovic

60

Club: *West Ham* **DOB:** *19/4/89*
Country: *Austria*

Some football experts were well surprised West Ham paid Stoke £25 million for Marko Arnautovic in 2017, but he silenced his critics with an awesome debut season for The Hammers! The Austria hitman bagged 11 Prem goals for West Ham in 2017-18!

Mariano

59

Club: *Real Madrid* **DOB:** *1/8/93*
Country: *Dominican Republic*

Mariano is one of Dominican Republic's greatest ever footy stars! He struggled to break into the first team during a five-year spell at Real Madrid, but after busting 18 Ligue 1 nets for Lyon in 2017-18, Real activated their buy-back option to re-sign the slick striker!

Ousmane Dembele

58

Club: *Barcelona* **DOB:** *15/5/97*

Country: *France*

Dembele sent shockwaves around Europe in 2017 with his £135.5 million move from Borussia Dortmund to Barça! He struggled big-time with injuries in his first season at the Spanish superclub, but his electric pace will light up the Nou Camp for years to come!

Bafetimbi Gomis

57

Club: *Al-Hilal* **DOB:** *6/8/85*

Country: *France*

The ex-Swansea striker is in the hottest form of his career! The powerful hitman helped Galatasaray win their first Turkish Super Lig title since 2014-15 after scoring an epic 29 league goals in 2017-18, and now he's on fire for Saudi Arabian champions Al-Hilal!

Moussa Marega

56

Club: *Porto* **DOB:** *14/4/91*

Country: *Mali*

Marega was Porto's top scorer in 2017-18. His 22 league goals helped The Dragons win their 28th Portuguese Primeira Liga trophy and fight off fierce rivals Benfica in an awesome title race. The Mali striker is famous for his defender-crushing power and finishing!

Florian Thauvin

55

Club: *Marseille* **DOB:** *26/1/93*

Country: *France*

Newcastle supporters might be shocked to see Thauvin in this list, but the France hero has improved loads since stinking up St. James' Park in 2015-16. Only Edinson Cavani scored more Ligue 1 goals than Thauvin in 2017-18 - he busted net 22 times!

Marcus Rashford

54

Club: *Man. Utd* **DOB:** *31/10/97*

Country: *England*

Wonderkid Rashford is one of the most exciting attacking talents in world footy! His confidence, pace and ability to score from all angles make him a proper scary opponent for defenders. Rashford has the potential to be 40 places higher in this list next year!

Cristhian Stuani

53

Club: *Girona DOB: 12/10/86*

Country: *Uruguay*

Stuani was the surprise star of La Liga in 2017-18. Following an up-and-down spell with Middlesbrough, he moved to Girona and helped his new club finish tenth in their first ever season in the Spanish top flight. He hit 21 goals to finish fifth in the scoring charts!

Aleksandr Kokorin

52

Club: *Zenit St. Petersburg*

Country: *Russia DOB: 19/3/91*

Kokorin's clever movement and mega slick finishing have made him one of the Russian Premier League's best strikers over the last ten years. Injury ended his dream of being Russia's main striker for the 2018 World Cup, but he has the class to be a future star!

Kevin Gameiro

51

Club: *Valencia DOB: 9/5/87*

Country: *France*

Gameiro burst onto the big stage with French club Lorient in 2009-10. Since then he's played for PSG, Sevilla, Atletico and Valencia, and he's one of the most consistent strikers in recent La Liga history - scoring 58 league goals in his last five full seasons. Legend!

Andre Silva

50

Club: *Sevilla DOB: 6/11/95*

Country: *Portugal*

Cristiano Ronaldo hogs all the headlines for Portugal, but Silva is one of the underrated superstars for the European champions. Rocket headers are his speciality and, after spells with Porto and AC Milan, he's now busting nets on loan at Spanish club Sevilla!

Aritz Aduriz

49

Club: *Athletic Bilbao*

Country: *Spain* DOB: 11/2/81

Athletic Bilbao's legendary striker is still destroying defenders and busting nets at the age of 37! Aduriz relies on his intelligent movement in the 18-yard box to bamboozle centre-backs and find space to finish. The golden oldie could be scoring for years to come!

Rodrigo

48

Club: *Valencia* DOB: 6/3/91

Country: *Spain*

Rodrigo has had a bonkers career playing for Real Madrid, Benfica and even Bolton, but now he's finally settled at Valencia! The 27-year-old was born in Brazil but plays for Spain and uses his speed to destroy defenders. He scored 16 La Liga goals in 2017-18!

Lorenzo Insigne

47

Club: *Napoli* DOB: 4/6/91

Country: *Italy*

There aren't many better attacking players in Serie A than Insigne right now. The 27-year-old has been ripping it up for years and is a major reason why Napoli are one of the most improved teams in Europe. The Italy ace loves cutting in from the left!

FACE IN THE CROWD

Can you spot these Premier League goal machines in this cool pic? There are ten to find!

Marko Arnautovic

Cenk Tosun

Jamie Vardy

Pierre-Emerick Aubameyang

Sergio Aguero

Harry Kane

Chris Wood

Romelu Lukaku

Glenn Murray

Mohamed Salah

WORDSEARCH

Find last season's Champions League top scorers in this grid!

Y	S	K	I																							K	B	B	J
Y	D	S	S																							B	E	J	Y
M	M	N	E																							C	N	Q	J
B	V	O	V																							P	Y	U	R
Y	X	I	S																							O	E	Y	O
S	N	V	U																							O	D	A	N
C	E	F	U	V	Q	J	Z	C	L	I	F	Z	M	U	G	Q	E	M	C	X	Y	I	M	V	G	A	D	D	A
I	Y	D	U	W	E	M	T	R	J	E	T	D	T	B	V	A	Q	S	J	Z	A	E	T	R	H	W	E	X	L
N	M	I	I	Y	F	N	R	S	U	T	K	G	M	P	V	N	H	A	W	V	L	B	X	J	Z	W	R	B	D
H	A	F	A	L	C	A	O	T	O	K	L	C	X	T	M	W	S	Y	Q	G	C	T	L	T	T	U	Q	X	O
A	R	M	D	S	L	W	W	U	O	E	I	K	B	E	X	V	B	N	W	U	Z	F	E	F	W	S	Y	A	O
R	V	F	C	H	H	A	Z	A	R	D	Y	M	G	B	A	J	X	T	P	V	Q	N	U	X	E	D	A	A	S
D	A	Z	N	E	D	R	X	O	Z	Y	S	K	M	F	R	A	M	A	N	D	Z	U	K	I	C	U	K	D	K
C	Y	S	J	G	E	I	U	H	U	D	H	N	R	I	J	A	Y	M	A	M	D	X	R	L	E	S	C	X	N
G	R	L	H	L	E	B	J	W	P	L	Z	E	F	S	C	I	U	W	Y	G	G	N	J	E	H	L	X	I	A
J	V	L	K	F	C	N	B	U	K	V	Z	K	N	F	J	H	D	O	N	B	I	Q	G	R	Q	I	X	J	S
H	P	K	S	G	O	M	D	C	W	R	Y	A	N	T	I	N	S	I	G	N	E	U	V	C	X	F	S	E	O
P	N	X	F	T	D	R	S	S	T	B	F	N	Q	G	I	T	L	E	W	A	N	D	O	W	S	K	I	Y	N
M	H	N	O	P	P	K	D	F	Y	Z	C	E	E	I	U	Z	F	V	S	K	X	D	B	N	M	X	H	A	W
C	G	J	B	R	Q	B	H	T	U	A	J	P	V	V	R	B	O	I	Q	S	S	F	H	I	G	T	Z	K	I
J	B	E	E	Z	Z	Q	N	G	K	B	D	D	O	L	I	Q	T	O	R	R	M	H	L	Q	V	V	W	K	Y
W	F	E	R	M	E	Z	R	H	B	J	T	B	E	N	Z	E	M	A	A	M	A	R	D	T	M	O	D	S	O
W	U	F	L	L	B	I	L	J	G	I	Z	L	U	K	A	K	U	X	T	L	I	U	X	R	B	H	G	N	O
S	E	F	I	P	Z	E	V	C	Y	U	H	V	V	G	Z	A	W	P	A	R	T	N	T	V	W	I	Y	X	Z
D	V	R	N	C	F	X	E	K	Z	H	V	H	C	G	T	D	K	S	C	S	D	H	O	W	U	G	N	M	D
O	X	I	N	G	B	Q	O	S	S	T	E	R	L	I	N	G	X	R	E	X	K	B	V	W	Z	U	M	L	X
L	S	W	F	E	J	M	W	K	W	Q	Q	S	S	Y	L	J	J	Q	A	Z	D	E	J	C	D	A	L	U	B
H	Z	K	T	C	R	Z	B	Q	N	A	G	L	P	P	T	R	U	N	Y	P	G	L	N	M	D	I	D	H	C
U	H	F	P	W	W	U	Z	M	E	S	S	I	D	H	J	C	O	U	P	F	O	D	J	V	C	N	Z	N	C
E	B	Q	I	T	O	W	K	F	U	B	Z	M	V	L	S	A	T	K	X	F	J	F	U	A	Y	Q	E	M	B
O	R	E	Q	E	Q	F	T	T	A	L	I	S	C	A	I	V	N	J	T	P	H	R	P	B	E	M	K	O	X
O	K	G	K	R	B	O	O	O	L	Y	I	C	D	Y	V	A	N	G	C	R	N	Z	J	O	S	M	O	W	K
M	C	P	L	S	I	G	H	S	D	F	F	L	T	Z	N	N	D	M	K	M	B	S	L	U	O	B	J	G	A
V	L	Q	E	V	U	N	U	P	O	H	R	N	B	E	X	I	L	N	C	A	A	X	I	B	S	A	K	T	G
O	X	R	Q	M	I	N	T	I	Y	O	D	X	X	P	S	N	Q	V	D	L	B	P	V	A	E	P	A	Q	U
X	H	R	B	T	X	A	G	G	N	L	S	D	H	S	H	K	G	U	H	U	B	R	Q	K	C	P	Y	J	E
U	F	K	U	O	D	X	C	B	H	V	P	N	U	G	I	H	K	M	R	H	Y	H	D	A	V	E	K	O	R
L	H	O	A	P	V	G	M	T	X	N	K	S	Z	S	T	I	V	B	Y	P	N	M	X	R	T	M	D	Q	O
Q	C	P	Z	Y	C	A	L	U	C	N	E	O	B	N	N	D	A	M	J	X	W	P	L	P	N	Z	J	K	S
Y	C	Y	M	A	N	E	B	Q	H	J	V	R	F	M	K	Z	E	N	Z	Z	X	O	I	W	U	C	L	J	Q

Aboubakar	Dzeko	Jesus	Mane	Ronaldo
Aguero	Falcao	Kane	Mbappe	Salah
Ben Yedder	Firmino	Kimmich	Messi	Son
Benzema	Hazard	Lewandowski	Neymar	Sterling
Cavani	Higuain	Lukaku	Oberlin	Talisca
Coutinho	Insigne	Mandzukic	Rashford	Werner

ANSWER ON PAGE

Dele Alli

46

Club: *Tottenham* **DOB:** *11/4/96*

Country: *England*

Dele Alli has a gift of being in the right place at the right time in the 18-yard box. Similar to Premier League legend Frank Lampard, Alli's clever movement gives him loads of goalscoring chances – and he usually takes them! The best is yet to come!

Cenk Tosun

45

Club: *Everton* **DOB:** *7/6/91*

Country: *Turkey*

Everton hitman Tosun is one of the deadliest finishers in the Prem. The Turkey striker was a proper legend at former club Besiktas, before earning a £27 million move to The Toffees last January. He made a big impact, scoring five goals before the end of the season!

Carlos Bacca

44

Club: *Villarreal* **DOB:** *8/9/86*

Country: *Colombia*

Bacca is back at Villarreal after two seasons at AC Milan and he's doing what he does best – busting La Liga nets for fun! The deadly Colombia striker has scored at least 13 league goals in each of the last six full seasons, including 15 for Villarreal in 2017-18. Wow!

Zlatan Ibrahimovic

43

Club: *LA Galaxy* **DOB:** *3/10/81*

Country: *Sweden*

Even nearing the end of his incredible career, Zlatan is still one of the most lethal strikers on the planet! The LA Galaxy ace mixes intelligence, natural talent, elite technique and massive confidence to make the ultimate goal king. Hero!

Thomas Muller

42

Club: *B. Munich* **DOB:** *13/9/89*

Country: *Germany*

What an unbelievable career Thomas Muller has had! He won the World Cup Golden Boot in 2010, bagged seven Bundesliga titles with Bayern Munich, lifted the World Cup with Germany in 2014, helped Bayern win the Champions League in 2013, plus more!

Eden Hazard

41

Club: *Chelsea* **DOB:** *7/1/91*

Country: *Belgium*

Hazard is more famous for his insane dribbling skills and crazy tricks, but he can also be a lethal finisher! The Belgium superstar scored 12 league goals in 2017-18 and 16 the season before to help Chelsea win their fifth Prem title!

Nils Petersen

40

Club: *Freiburg* **DOB:** *6/12/88*

Country: *Germany*

Nils Petersen was a massive breakout star of the Bundesliga in 2017-18 after he finished second in the top scorer charts behind Bayern Munich striker Robert Lewandowski. Freiburg were in a relegation scrap all season, but Petersen's goals helped his team stay up!

Gareth Bale

39

Club: *Real Madrid*

Country: *Wales* **DOB:** *16/7/89*

The Welsh wonder grabbed the headlines in 2018 after scoring one of the greatest goals in footy history! Bale's stunning overhead kick for Real Madrid against Liverpool in the Champions League final showcased his raw talent and mind-blowing technique!

Karim Benzema

38

Club: *Real Madrid*

Country: *France* **DOB:** *19/12/87*

Benzema has been one of the most consistent strikers in world football over the last ten years. His unselfish style up front helped former Real Madrid team-mate Cristiano Ronaldo reach his full potential, but he's also netted plenty of epic net-busters himself!

Iago Aspas

37

Club: *Celta Vigo* **DOB:** *1/8/87*

Country: *Spain*

Liverpool fans won't believe what a fantastic player Iago Aspas has turned into! The Spain hitman didn't have much success at Anfield, but he's back in La Liga with Celta Vigo and making goalkeepers look silly! He smashed home 22 league goals last season!

Jonas

36

Club: *Benfica* **DOB:** *1/4/84*

Country: *Brazil*

Jonas has got to be the most underrated striker in Europe! The Benfica legend rarely gets linked with big-money transfers and doesn't get the same hype as other Primeira Liga stars, but his stats are epic. He scored 34 goals in just 30 games in 2017-18!

Mario Mandzukic

35

Club: *Juventus* **DOB:** *21/5/86*

Country: *Croatia*

Mandzukic has showcased his talents at some of Europe's biggest clubs, including Juve, Atletico Madrid and Bayern Munich. He's scored in two Champions League finals as well, including an outrageous overhead kick in the 2017 final against Real Madrid!

Alvaro Morata

34

Club: *Chelsea* **DOB:** *23/10/92*

Country: *Spain*

You won't find many strikers who can head the ball as well as Alvaro Morata. The Chelsea striker's technique, bravery and power make him one of football's greatest heading heroes. He's good with his feet too, and has busted nets for Real Madrid and Juventus!

STAT ATTACK!

50

In 2011-12, Lionel Messi scored 50 La Liga goals in just 36 starts for Barça. How mad is that?

2

Robert Lewandowski scored two Bundesliga hat-tricks in March 2018. He bagged ace trebles for Bayern Munich against Hamburg and Borussia Dortmund. Sweet!

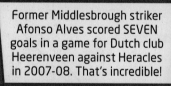

5

Juventus players hit five Serie A hat-tricks in 2017-18. There were three for Paulo Dybala, one for Gonzalo Higuain and a shock treble from DM Sami Khedira!

7

Former Middlesbrough striker Afonso Alves scored SEVEN goals in a game for Dutch club Heerenveen against Heracles in 2007-08. That's incredible!

13

Pierre-Emerick Aubameyang finished sixth in the 2017-18 Bundesliga scoring charts with 13 goals, despite leaving Borussia Dortmund to join Arsenal halfway through the season!

18

Kilmarnock ace Kris Boyd won the Scottish Premiership top scorer prize in 2017-18. His 18 goals were eight more than any Celtic player. Unbelievable!

7

Atletico Madrid hero Antoine Griezmann scored seven La Liga goals in just four days in 2017-18! He netted a hat-trick against Sevilla on February 25, then four past Leganes on February 28!

28

PSG's all-time top goalscorer Edinson Cavani finished 2017-18 as the leading goal-grabber in France with 28 Ligue 1 goals!

8

Lazio superstar Ciro Immo and Athletic Bilbao striker Aduriz were joint-top scor the Europa League in 201 with eight goals each. He

38

Lionel Messi top scorer in L history! By the the 2017-18 the Barcelo had hit 383

34

Benfica legend Jonas proved his shooting boots were more lethal than ever by winning the Portuguese Primeira Liga top scorer award in 2017-18 with 34 net-busters!

Michy Batshuayi

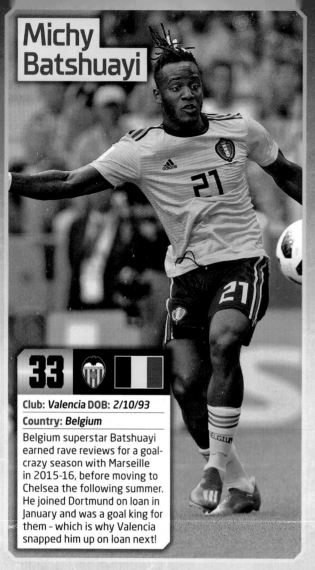

33

Club: *Valencia* **DOB:** *2/10/93*

Country: *Belgium*

Belgium superstar Batshuayi earned rave reviews for a goal-crazy season with Marseille in 2015-16, before moving to Chelsea the following summer. He joined Dortmund on loan in January and was a goal king for them – which is why Valencia snapped him up on loan next!

Radamel Falcao

32

Club: *Monaco* **DOB:** *10/2/86*

Country: *Colombia*

Colombia's record goalscorer Falcao is one of their greatest footy stars of all time! His form dipped after a red-hot run at Porto and Atletico Madrid, but his career got back on track in 2016 with a move to Monaco, where he scored 39 league goals in just two seasons!

Olivier Giroud

31

Club: *Chelsea* **DOB:** *30/9/86*

Country: *France*

Giroud joined Chelsea in January 2018 after six seasons with Arsenal. The France striker's clever finishing has helped him become one of the Prem's best forwards, and he won the FIFA Puskas Award in 2017 for his legendary scorpion kick goal against Crystal Palace!

Heung-min Son

30

Club: *Tottenham* **DOB:** *8/7/92*

Country: *South Korea*

Speedster Son is finally getting the credit he deserves after a series of epic performances for Tottenham. The South Korea hero is one of the best attacking wide players in the Premier League and hurts defenders with his direct playing style and energy!

Sadio Mane

29

Club: *Liverpool* **DOB:** *10/4/92*

Country: *Senegal*

Liverpool have turned into one of the best attacking teams on the planet – and Mane is a big part of their success! He scored in every knockout round of the Champo League last season, including a hat-trick in the last 16 and a class goal in the final!

Alexandre Lacazette

27

Club: *Arsenal* **DOB:** *28/5/91*

Country: *France*

Lacazette is one of Europe's best penalty-box predators. Some of his numbers are insane, with 28 Ligue 1 goals for Lyon in 2016-17, 21 in 2015-16 and 27 in 2014-15, before bagging 14 Premier League strikes in his debut season with Arsenal. Class!

Marco Reus

28

Club: *B. Dortmund* **DOB:** *31/5/89*

Country: *Germany*

Injuries have stopped Marco Reus becoming a Ballon d'Or contender in recent seasons, but he's still an awesome player to watch when he's fit and on top form. His finishing style is very tough to stop, with dribbles down the left and finesse-style shooting!

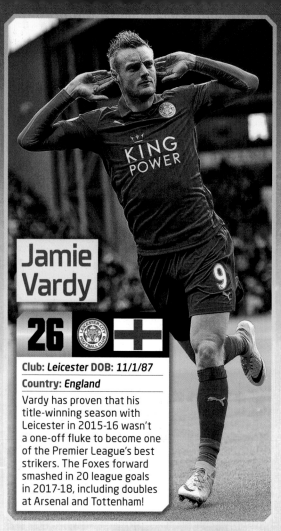

Alexis Sanchez

25

Club: *Man. United*
Country: *Chile* **DOB:** *19/12/88*

Alexis Sanchez is everything you want from a modern-day forward – energetic, skilful, aggressive and full of goals! The way he shifts the ball from the left wing onto his favourite right foot is tough for defenders to stop – and it leads to plenty of goals!

Jamie Vardy

26

Club: *Leicester* **DOB:** *11/1/87*
Country: *England*

Vardy has proven that his title-winning season with Leicester in 2015-16 wasn't a one-off fluke to become one of the Premier League's best strikers. The Foxes forward smashed in 20 league goals in 2017-18, including doubles at Arsenal and Tottenham!

Timo Werner

24

Club: *RB Leipzig* **DOB:** *6/3/96*
Country: *Germany*

Leipzig became a Bundesliga superclub in 2016-17 – and Werner was their star player! His mind-blowing pace made them well devastating on the counter-attack and he quickly became Germany's main No.9 too. He's a future legend!

Gabriel Jesus

23

Club: *Man. City* **DOB:** *3/4/97*

Country: *Brazil*

Man. City beat loads of top clubs to sign Gabriel Jesus from Palmeiras in 2017 and he's rapidly turning into one of Pep Guardiola's star players. His top skill is movement and it helps him find space in the box for tons of scoring chances. His finishing totally rules, too!

Roberto Firmino

22

Club: *Liverpool* **DOB:** *2/10/91*

Country: *Brazil*

Liverpool's silky Brazil forward is one of the most improved footy stars on the planet. He's an unselfish team player, but can also be well lethal in front of goal at the right moment. Firmino bagged 15 Prem goals in 2017-18, plus another ten in the Champions League!

Kylian Mbappe

21

Club: *PSG* **DOB:** *20/12/98*

Country: *France*

The sky is the limit for PSG wonderkid Kylian Mbappe! The speedy France forward could easily be in the top five of our countdown next year, because his footy potential is unlimited! Mbappe was one of the stars of World Cup 2018 and could help PSG rule Europe next!

Raheem Sterling

20

Club: Man. City **DOB:** 8/12/94

Country: *England*

Sterling has turned into an elite forward under manager Pep Guardiola at Man. City. He always had electric pace and mad dribbling skills, but he's improved his movement and finishing big-time! Raheem smashed in 18 Prem goals in 2017-18 – that's world-class!

Ciro Immobile

19

Club: *Lazio* **DOB:** *20/2/90*

Country: *Italy*

Immobile had a massive dip in his scoring stats when he left Italy, but he moved back to his home country in 2016 and it was a career-changing decision! He netted 23 Serie A goals for Lazio in 2016-17, then went even better in 2017-18 with 29 strikes. He's mega lethal!

Dries Mertens

18

Club: *Napoli* **DOB:** *6/5/87*

Country: *Belgium*

The Napoli ace played most of his career as a winger, but he's turned into a deadly striker over the last few seasons in Serie A. He can still score epic goals like his stunner in the World Cup for Belgium against Panama, but his main strength is his one-on-one finishing!

Romelu Lukaku

17

Club: *Man. United* **DOB:** *13/5/93*

Country: *Belgium*

Man. United paid Everton a wallet-busting £75 million for Romelu Lukaku in 2017, and he's repaid them with some top-quality performances. The powerful striker scored 16 Prem goals in his debut season at Old Trafford, then rocked the 2018 World Cup!

Diego Costa

16

Club: *Atletico Madrid*

Country: *Spain* **DOB:** *7/10/88*

Diego Costa has his critics everywhere he goes, but he always silences them with incredible performances and loads of goals. He also proved he should be Spain's main striker with an epic double against Portugal at the World Cup. His passion is awesome!

STAT ATTACK!

19

Kylian Mbappe was the youngest goalscorer at the 2018 World Cup. The France ace scored against Peru aged 19 years and 183 days. Wow!

3

England legend Geoff Hurst scored a famous hat-trick in the 1966 World Cup final. He's the only player in history to bag a treble in the final!

15

Brazil icon Ronaldo scored 15 World Cup goals in just 19 games during his epic career!

13

France legend Just Fontaine holds the record for most goals in a single World Cup. He hit 13 in just six games at the 1958 tournament!

5

Oleg Salenko is the only player ever to score five goals in a single World Cup game. He did it for Russia against Cameroon in 1994!

8

Golden Boot winners scored exactly six goals at every World Cup between 1978 and 1998, before Brazil ace Ronaldo's eight strikes at the 2002 World Cup!

1986

Harry Kane became the first England player to net a World Cup hat-trick since Gary Lineker in 1986, when he buried three past Panama!

16

Miroslav Klose is the top scorer in World Cup history! The German hit 16 goals over four tournaments!

4

Four heroes finished World Cup 2010 on five goals – David Villa, Thomas Muller, Diego Forlan and Wesley Sneijder!

2

Argentina legend Gabriel Batistuta is the only player ever to score hat-tricks at two World Cups. He bagged trebles in the 1994 and 1998 tournaments!

3

Cristiano Ronaldo only hit three goals at the 2006, 2010 and 2014 World Cups combined, before doubling his tally with a sick hat-trick in his first game of the 2018 tournament against Spain!

Mauro Icardi

15

Club: *Inter* **DOB:** *19/2/93*

Country: *Argentina*

Icardi finished 2017-18 as joint-top scorer in Serie A with Lazio striker Ciro Immobile. His 29 league goals helped Inter qualify for the Champions League group stage for the first time since 2011-12, and now he's ready to totally own Europe's best defenders!

Paulo Dybala

14

Club: *Juventus* **DOB:** *15/11/93*

Country: *Argentina*

Dybala has already won three Serie A titles with Juve and there are clearly loads more trophies to come! He scored 22 league goals in 2017-18 and knocked Tottenham out of the Champo League with a class finish at Wembley!

Antoine Griezmann

13

Club: *Atletico Madrid*

Country: *France* **DOB:** *21/3/91*

Atletico's star player is in the hottest form of his life! He won Euro 2016's Golden Boot, hit 79 La Liga goals in his last four full seasons, scored an ace match-winning double in the 2018 Europa League final and then bagged in the World Cup final!

Edin Dzeko

12

Club: *Roma* **DOB:** *17/3/86*

Country: *Bosnia & Herzegovina*

Dzeko's enjoyed an epic career – and it's nowhere near over yet! The powerful striker has scored 14 or more league goals in seven different seasons, including 16 Serie A strikes for Roma in 2017-18, plus eight more in the Champo League!

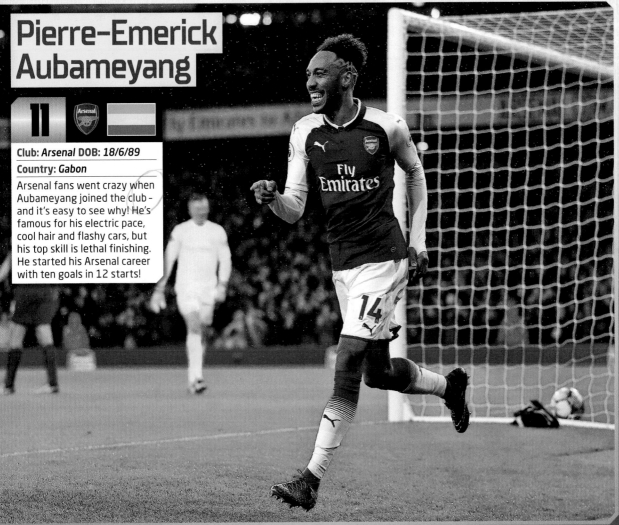

Pierre-Emerick Aubameyang

11

Club: *Arsenal* **DOB:** *18/6/89*

Country: *Gabon*

Arsenal fans went crazy when Aubameyang joined the club – and it's easy to see why! He's famous for his electric pace, cool hair and flashy cars, but his top skill is lethal finishing. He started his Arsenal career with ten goals in 12 starts!

Sergio Aguero

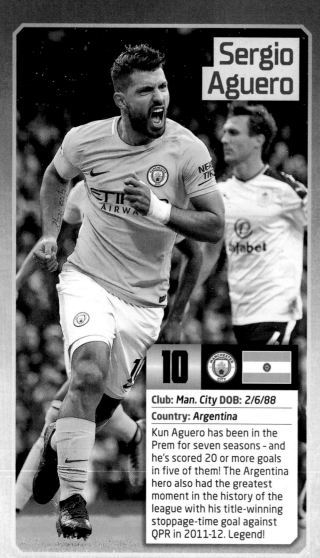

10

Club: *Man. City* **DOB:** *2/6/88*

Country: *Argentina*

Kun Aguero has been in the Prem for seven seasons – and he's scored 20 or more goals in five of them! The Argentina hero also had the greatest moment in the history of the league with his title-winning stoppage-time goal against QPR in 2011-12. Legend!

Gonzalo Higuain

9

Club: *AC Milan* **DOB:** *10/12/87*

Country: *Argentina*

Some experts were shocked when Juventus splashed out £75.3 million to sign Higuain from Napoli in 2016, but he was worth every single penny! He scored 40 league goals in just two seasons for The Old Lady, before making a shock loan move to rivals AC Milan!

Neymar

8

Club: *PSG* **DOB:** *5/2/92*

Country: *Brazil*

Neymar is one of the most naturally talented footballers in history. The Brazil trickster netted a cool 19 Ligue 1 goals in just 20 starts for PSG in 2017-18. He's already scored in one Champions League final and is targeting loads more success in 2018-19. Class!

Edinson Cavani

7

PARIS SAINT-GERMAIN · *URUGUAY*

Club: *PSG* **DOB:** *14/2/87*

Country: *Uruguay*

Cavani is one of the hardest working No.9s in world footy! His aggression and energy are epic to watch, but he's lethal in front of goal too. His double v Portugal at the World Cup was legendary, and proof he's unstoppable on his best form!

Harry Kane

6

TOTTENHAM · *ENGLAND*

Club: *Tottenham* **DOB:** *28/7/93*

Country: *England*

Harry Kane scores goals. Lots of them! The lethal Tottenham striker was the Prem's shock star in 2014-15 with 21 goals, then went on to score 25 in 2015-16, 29 in 2016-17 and 30 in 2017-18. Then he won the Golden Boot at the 2018 World Cup. What a total ledge!

FOOTY MIS-MATCH

Check out these two pics, then see if you can spot the ten differences between them!

GOAL MACHINES BRAIN-BUSTER

Can you pick up a perfect score in our goal machines quiz?

1. Which massive MLS club did Premier League legend Wayne Rooney join last summer?

2. Harry Kane finished second to which player in the 2017-18 Premier League Golden Boot race?

3. Who scored a hat-trick during Portugal and Spain's 3-3 draw at the 2018 World Cup?

4. Which huge Yorkshire city was awesome Leicester goal machine Jamie Vardy born?

5. Which Premier League ace scored for South Korea against Germany at the 2018 World Cup?

6. Who won the Ligue 1 top scorer prize in 2017-18 – Neymar or Edinson Cavani?

7. Matej Vydra was the top scorer with 21 goals in which awesome league in 2017-18?

8. Samba superstar Gabriel Jesus joined Man. City from which Brazilian club in 2017?

9. How many goals did Belgium's Romelu Lukaku score in the group stage of the 2018 World Cup?

10. Barcelona signed Ousmane Dembele from which massive Bundesliga club in 2017?

1 ....
2 ....
3 ....
4 ....
5 ....
6 ....
7 ....
8 ....
9 ....
10 ....

ANSWER ON PAGE

Robert Lewandowski

5

Club: *Bayern Munich*

Country: *Poland* **DOB:** *21/8/88*

Lewa has been ripping nets for years, but defenders still can't work out how to stop him! The Bayern megastar has scored 89 Bundesliga goals in his last three full seasons, and he's the only player in history to score four goals in a Champo League semi-final game. Legendary!

DID YOU KNOW?

Lewandowski has only failed to score over 20 league goals in a season once since 2011!

Luis Suarez

4

Club: *Barcelona* **DOB:** *24/1/87*

Country: *Uruguay*

Suarez's career has been crazy, but everyone knows he's an awesome striker! The Uruguay legend hammered 31 goals in 33 Prem games for Liverpool in 2013-14, before earning a £65 million move to Barcelona! Since then he's bagged over 100 La Liga goals for them!

DID YOU KNOW?

Suarez won the European Golden Shoe in 2013–14 and 2015–16. Hero!

Mohamed Salah

3

Club: *Liverpool*

Country: *Egypt* **DOB:** *15/6/92*

Liverpool fans found a new hero in 2017-18 and his name is Mohamed Salah. From the first Prem game of the season against Watford, they knew their club had bought a special player. His pace and dribbling have been epic for years, but now he's finishing like a star!

DID YOU KNOW?

Salah spent 2014 to 2016 at Premier League rivals Chelsea, but only made six league starts in two seasons!

Cristiano Ronaldo

2

Club: *Juventus* **DOB:** *5/2/85*

Country: *Portugal*

Quite simply one of the best players in footy history, CR7 can do it all. The Juventus icon has been the top goalscorer in the Champions League seven times, won five Ballon d'Or awards and scored over 30 league goals in a season seven times. Cristiano's too good!

DID YOU KNOW?

Cristiano Ronaldo has played in six Champions League finals and scored in three of them!

Lionel Messi

1

Club: *Barcelona* **DOB:** *24/6/87*

Country: *Argentina*

Messi is No.1 in our countdown after another epic season and one of the greatest careers in footy history! The Argentina hero won his fifth European Golden Shoe in 2017-18 after scoring 34 La Liga goals. He's also won nine Spanish titles and four Champions Leagues!

TURN OVER!
Check out loads of mind-blowing Messi stats and facts on the next page!

STAT ATTACK!

LIONEL MESSI

You've seen our Top 100 Goal Machines. Now check out why Lionel Messi is top of our list!

73 Leo holds the all-time record for most goals in a season after ripping up 2011-12. He bagged a mind-blowing 73 goals in all competitions!

10 The Argentina icon netted ten goals in just 12 starts during the South American qualifying rounds for the 2014 World Cup!

Messi smashed in 96 La Liga goals in just 64 starts during the 2011-12 and 2012-13 seasons combined. Will we ever see stats like that again? **96**

5 He's won La Liga's top scorer prize five times, including the 2017-18 season after his 34 goals!

2014 Messi won the Golden Ball for being player of the tournament at the 2014 World Cup!

He hasn't scored less than 23 league goals in a season since 2007-08. Most players would be happy scoring that many in one season. Legend! **23**

2

Leo has scored in two Champions League finals. His first was a sick header against Man. United in 2009, then a powerful strike against the same club two years later. Hero!

26

He holds the record for most goals in games between Barcelona and Real Madrid. By the end of 2017-18, he'd bagged 26 El Clasico goals!

5

The Argentina forward has won five Ballon d'Or awards in his awesome career, including four in a row between 2009 and 2012!

#MESSI5

8

Messi scored an incredible eight hat-tricks in La Liga during the 2011/12 season!

5

Messi has scored nine or more goals in a Champions League season five times in his career, including 14 in the 2011-12 competition!

COMPETITION

OLLIE WATKINS
Brentford

MARTYN WAGHORN
Derby

LEON CLARKE
Sheffield United

JAY RODRIGUEZ
West Brom

You've seen our Top 100, but there are loads of net-busters in the EFL Championship too! Pick your Top 5 for the chance to win an ace prize!

WIN! HYPERVENOMS

Just pick your favourite five goal kings from the EFL Championship. If your five are the same as MATCH's five in any order, then your name will go into the draw to win a pair of Nike Hypervenom boots - thanks to our mates at Sports Direct. Good luck!

SPORTS DIRECT

Boot colourway may vary from picture shown and is subject to availability.

CHAMPIONSHIP GOAL KINGS!

ALBERT ADOMAH
Aston Villa

BRITT ASSOMBALONGA
Middlesbrough

BENIK AFOBE
Stoke

Write down your top five Championship goal kings, fill out your details and send a photocopy of this page to:
Goal Machines 2019, MATCH Magazine, Kelsey Media, Regent House, Welbeck Way, Peterborough, Cambridgeshire, PE2 7WH
Closing date: January 31, 2019.

1.

2.

3.

4.

5.

NAME: Celyn Davies

DATE OF BIRTH: 29/05/2010

ADDRESS:

MOBILE:

EMAIL:

BOOT SIZE:

Face In The Crowd P28

Wordsearch P29

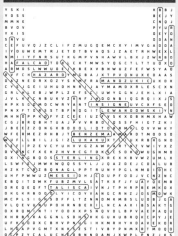

Brain-Buster P49

1. DC United
2. Mohamed Salah
3. Cristiano Ronaldo
4. Sheffield
5. Heung-min Son
6. Edinson Cavani
7. EFL Championship
8. Palmeiras
9. Four
10. Borussia Dortmund

Footy Mis-Match P48

LOVE MATCH?
GET IT DELIVERED EVERY WEEK!

15 FREE POSTERS

GOALS & STATS! STAR MEN & MORE!

HUGE MATCH REPORTS! Every single World Cup game covered!

MATCH!

WORLD CUP POSTER PULLOUT

RUSSIA 2018 COOL POSTERS

ENGLAND v BELGIUM! Trippier & Hazard talk to MATCH!

COME ON ENGLAND!

WE'RE SUPPORTING THE THREE LIONS ALL THE WAY!

WIN!

VE-BUSTERS! ...ford, Liverpool and loads more new kits!

SICK SKILLS Play like Lingard!

PLUS! ► FREE ACADEMY TRIAL ► QUIZZES ► FIFA 18 BATTLE – KANE v LUKAKU!

4 ISSUES FOR JUST £1!*

PACKED EVERY WEEK WITH...

★ Red-hot gear
★ FIFA tips
★ Stats & quizzes
★ Massive stars
★ Posters & pics
& loads more!

STRIKE LIKE SALAH!

MATCH! ACADEMY Play like the stars!

ITK RACE FOR THE... GOLDEN SHOE! MAKES YOU IN THE KNOW EVERY SINGLE WEEK

ITK EPIC KICKS

KUN'S WC WEAPONS!